T0124738

Out of the
DARKNESS

Out of the
DARKNESS

A BOOK OF THOUGHTS

TIMOTHY MAHFOOD

Editors:
Cayce Mollycheck
Laurie E. Teleford Mahfood
Jay Mahfood

iUniverse LLC
Bloomington

OUT OF THE DARKNESS
A Book of Thoughts

iUniverse books may be ordered through booksellers or by contacting:

iUniverse LLC
1663 Liberty Drive
Bloomington, IN 47403
www.iuniverse.com
1-800-Authors (1-800-288-4677)

Because of the dynamic nature of the Internet, any web addresses or
links contained in this book may have changed since publication and
may no longer be valid. The views expressed in this work are solely those
of the author and do not necessarily reflect the views of the publisher,
and the publisher hereby disclaims any responsibility for them.

Any people depicted in stock imagery provided by Thinkstock are models,
and such images are being used for illustrative purposes only.
Certain stock imagery © Thinkstock.

ISBN: 978-1-4917-3123-9 (sc)
ISBN: 978-1-4917-3124-6 (e)

Library of Congress Control Number: 2014908602

Printed in the United States of America.

iUniverse rev. date: 05/07/2014

Dedicated to my Grandfather

Ferdinand Mahfood

Founder of Food for the Poor

The Candle in My Darkness

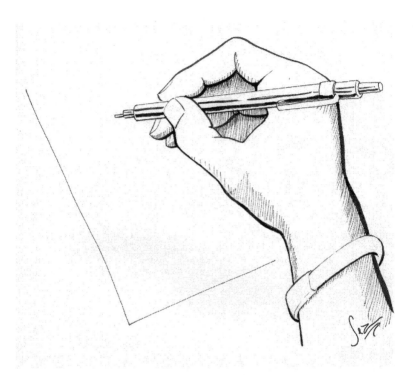

"Hand Writing"
By Sean Henry

Been a While

Been a while since I last touched this pen,
But you forced it out again.

Poetry, my dark thoughts compiled into one,
These pages weep inside me becoming a time bomb,
So the ink can spread inside of me.
Defined by one hateful remark,
I have to stay down,
Measuring my worth with how you describe me,

Just like how it used to be, again.

Keep it Hidden

I'm sitting on the side of this cliff
Looking down into the emptiness,
I know I am alone, but what if
I was not so damn hideous.

Maybe I should not have gotten up today
And all of a sudden
I stand up and try to keep these feelings at bay,
I need to keep them hidden.

'Cause I can't let anyone see them,
Need to pretend to be dreaming of going far.
But that's why you are reading this poem,
Even though it seems so bizarre.

But I can't guarantee
That I won't just recede.

"Chillin on the Cliff"
By Sean Henry

Ink

Words etched blankly on a paper,
Without feeling or love.
Ink fades away depressingly,
And paper stains away and loses life.

I try desperately to write something close to the heart,
But it comes out a lie.
Real thoughts like "why bother" and
    "what's the point" fill my head.
It leaves this paper halfway done
And my ink left sad and unused.
I'll give up and turn my back on the thing
    that holds me together.

Because there are no colors other than black I can see,
And I feel so alone,
Running in the same spot,
Trying to escape from the monsters I hold secretly.
This ink leaks from my eyes,
And leaves stains in the open.
For me to always remember.

Shoulder

I have a demon up on my shoulder,
And as I get older,
My dreams get darker.

I used to have a saint on my shoulder,
He said he was sorry,
He had the way, but my head is stubborn.

Now I want to sell my soul,
But it ain't worth ***** to no one.

"Devil on my Shoulder"
By Sean Henry

Monsters

The grass I step on will wilt and never grow, no colors ever show.
There are monsters, hidden in this place.
But these monsters I hold.

They claw through my heart, begging for air.
I have held them in for too long.

I continue to battle them. I feel like I'm lost in this place.
I want to leave but I'm too scared to move.
For I might scare you and I fear you will go.

Nothing left inside but a name, I want to
     live my life to be with you,
But there is something creeping beneath my skin.

Now these monsters, I hope, will leave
I've never been strongly religious but I pray to God,
To remove this pain and make it leave.
Your name will never leave my heart, and I will
     never let these monsters touch it.
But these sadistic monsters I keep locked inside,
Will end up killing me and I fear they might touch you.
Something I can never let them do.

Falling

It's times like this when I sit and think,
Who would really miss me if I left for good?
Would anybody care or just shrug it off?
It feels like I can barely breathe.

So I will get liquored up and go for a walk,
And I will end up in the same place as I always do,
Standing on this roof looking at the view.

There is no way out for me.
This is my last breath.

I put one foot over the edge and the other follows suit.
I'm finally free.

"I'm Finally Free"
By Tamara Lewis

Darkness

The darkness inside me has been growing,
Not even the light from you can pierce its veil,
From the look on your face I can tell you
    have seen my dark wing,
While it pierces the skin and my faces goes pale.

My eyes turn black along with my soul,
I am no longer one of your kind.
It seems my hatred has taken toll,
I have lost control.

Shame passes through my heart,
As I realize what I have done;
I attempt to regain control over myself and it rips me apart,
I have tainted myself now, forever I am blackened.

My pulse stops and the transformation is complete,
I am now forever a dark angel.

"Dark Angel"
By Sean Henry

Fading

Fade away,
Run from the light and escape the sound,
Venture far into the dark,
And enjoy the silence.

But how long can I run,
And act like it's no big deal;
Someday I will find out.

I'm just sick of the shadows,
Looking for a spark to reignite.

No regrets, no limits this time.

Wondering

What's the point of being so alone?
It's what makes me sick inside.
Running away is something I can't condone,
So I'll search for where my pain resides.

The feeling cuts through me,
Like a rusty blade.
It'll leave a mark you'll see,
And send me to an early grave.

This emotion is like a sea of black arrows,
Sailing through the wind,
They leave me stiff as a scarecrow,
When will this end?

Cross my heart and swear to die,
The end is nowhere nearby.

"Razor Blade"
By Tamarra Kirkpatrick

Pictures

In my head,
The mental pictures flow,
Strange images you couldn't comprehend.

Fragmented into thousands,
I search to gather them all,
But I cannot seem to piece them together.

It's just like corrupt data,
In a computer's memory,
But it cannot be forgotten in a click.

I can only look forward,
To add new pictures,
That might not be corrupted.

Hurts

There is no explanation for
Why it hurts to be alive,
Why it's like this,
I just want to sever these ties.

I've given up,
Sick of these things,
Ashamed of myself,
I am a stranger to what this world brings

With no one to hold my hand,
I just want to go far away.
I have loved too much,
So I'll die young this day.

Paranoia

This paranoia is trapping me like a ghost;
I see spirits all around me,
But I don't want to be the host.
They're on a scaring spree:
Before I die I want to be free,
Oh, the life I lead,
I just need to see,
This sacred plea: it's killing me, oh the things I see,
So paint my portrait, they're right below my knee,
I feel denigrated
Oh the webs I weave,
Maybe I will be able to leave.

"Surrounded by Spirits"
By Romario Dunn

Trapped

I am stained by things I've done,
I try to hide from them,
But they chase and I cannot outrun,
They slowly pull me to requiem.

Depression has sung eternally,
The hate hangs in the notes.
Driving me to insanity,
The pain is so cutthroat.

Falling through the darkness,
The despair pulls me down with its weight.
It eats at me and leaves me lifeless,
But the pain slowly abates.

I am afraid to feel,
Anything that's real.

Rain

Memories shatter like glass,
Near impossible to put back together,
With sharp edges and names on brass,
They get swept away by rainy weather.

This pain has taken its toll,
Not sure how much more I can take.
These scars will mark my soul,
And my resolve is about to break.

I was always sad,
But you used to make me glad to be alive.
Now that you're gone how am I supposed to conquer the bad?
Will my happiness ever be able to revive?

It's gotten to the point where even you can't stop the pain,
But hopefully the bad will be washed away
    and the good will remain.

Confusion in My Brain

Shall I trust them and show them my phoniness,
Or trust no one and live in loneliness.
I can't hold on.
There's too much pain.
With thoughts of suicide in my brain,
Confusing my every action;
I wish it were a simple chore to face my demons.
One man shouldn't be alone,
Should I fight the pain? Or surrender my arms?
Do I trust them? Or live in loneliness?
My feelings can't be right, someone give me the courage to fight,
Or I will be sucked into this maelstrom of pain.

Dark Side of the Moon

On the dark side of the moon,
I wonder what lies in our close proximity.
Will it hold forces wrapped in stellar cocoons?
Strange creatures of anonymity?

Who knows what we will find,
Strange spiritual entities?
Our race just cannot intellectually rend,
Or just structures with no identity?

Maybe just a race with no severity,
With no potential harm to our future?
Or another species further along in evolutional reality,
Than we could ever mentally picture?

It truly is a terrifying yet exciting thing to imagine,
Hopefully it will be something we can fathom.

First published work by Timothy Mahfood in 2012 at age 15
In the book "Stars in Our Hearts: Facets"
By the World Poetry Movement.

"Moon"
By K.M.M.

Words

Spray the words throughout the halls,
Scream them at the top of your lungs.
Through the echo we hear the call,
And because of our braveness it overcomes.

I don't wanna believe the words,
But they seep through and thicken my blood.
Like heavy baggage,
I'm pulled by the flood.

But when I'm gone,
Keep spreading the **words,**
Keep singing the same song,
Until they're all cured.

"Spray Can"
By Sean Henry

Leave or stay

The look in your eyes is scaring me,
But it gets worse when you scream at me.

And what if I tell,
That your anger is trapping me up inside?

Would you care
If I disappeared?
Let me say this one more time

"If you leave I won't follow you,
But if you stay, I will always be with you.

So take my hand or walk away."

Out of the Darkness

I remember the melancholy days.
That always lingers in my mind.
I remember Grandpa's words
which left me in a daze,

And also
helped me
become unconfined.

Stuck with a feeling of loneliness,
He took me in a room to talk.
He gave me a feeling of braveness,
I remembered his words around the clock.

He told me of his past,
Something he mentioned
Tore out the loneliness
From me, at last!

I no longer felt alone
inside my world
of second dimension.

Because he has felt the same as me.
Inside his heart he also remembers melancholy days.
He took me "**Out of the Darkness**",
With his skeleton key.

He is the Candle in my Darkness
That has set my sadness ablaze.

"Out of the Darkness"
By Alana Igbe

Help

He tells her his problems,
Expecting to be comforted by soft lies.
She says his problems make her mind ache,
That he is just a liar
Expecting attention.
But what if that's all he wanted?

"A Couple Talking"
by Lahayma Robinson age 14

"A Note"
by Lahayma Robinson age 14

A few days pass,
And she hasn't heard from him in a while.
One day she finds a note under her door that reads
"Screw this place, I hate you all.
I thought you might want to know,
This is the end for me, whether you care or not.
I'll never see you again".
And the girl thinks he is joking.

"Heartbroken"
by Karieta Robinson age 17

A few days later,
The boy was not joking,
And ended up killing himself.
The girl was heartbroken,
Thought it was all her fault,
And took her own life in a spiral of depression.

This may be metaphorical,
But make sure
You don't make the same mistake.
If a friend comes looking for help, help him.
Regardless of how he has treated you.
Not trying to help someone
Who is about to write a suicide note
Is that not the same as having his blood on your hands?

"Reaching Out"
by Karieta Robinson age 17

Voices

Why do I have these twisted thoughts?
They leave me stretched out like a used rubber band.
I must beware of the voices inside my head,
My instincts tell me to act fast . . . when I can.

But I'm too scared to move,
Can't you help me, Miss?
The voices echo within my skull,
Steering me into madness.

Every word and every action are controlled by the voices.
Even though I want to try, and search for an answer.
Should I just give up to this madness?
Or should I be forced to surrender?

Her Again

I was up on a ledge
About to jump,
But it was you who pledged
To save me from the dump.

When the ground around me was collapsing
And I was searching for my savior,
It was you again who got me balancing,
And pulled me skyward.

And when I had this razor clenched in my fist,
About to end my life.
It was you, who pulled it from my wrist,
And now in my heart love is rife.

Please stay with me forever,
I can't live without you Tamara.

"A Sketch of Tammy"
by K.M.M.

My Sunshine

When you tell me you love me,
It sends shivers down my spine.
You found the key to this heart,
And changed who I used to be.

When you're gone, it makes me ache.
I know I walked astray,
And I know I made mistakes,
But you helped me find my way.

It used to hurt to be a man,
But you gave me an outlet for my feelings.
You give me a reason to be happy,
And saved me from myself.

"You are my sunshine,
My only sunshine."

You

You gotta tell me
The secret you hold,
Gotta tell me
All of the untold.

Rise off your knee,
Give your soul what it needs.
Off your knee,
And plant the seed.

Fight against the pain,
Break the chain,
Against the pain,
Run through the rain.

Cover your eyes,
Hide them from the lies.

This Love

Your smile is the only thing I need,
Anything with you I can see.
You've healed me up and I can't believe
You have stayed with me.
Just the smell of you
Makes me go crazy.
Now I am in this position,
What should I do?
Is it cool if I hold your hand?
Would you mind if I kiss you?
How would you feel if you knew this was about you?
I ask myself this all the time.
I give my heart to you,
But with the feeling of failing inside
Anxiety building in my mind,
I wanna take this chance.
I hope you will take my hand,
Because I want to stay close to you.
How long have I waited to tell you how I feel?

"Hands Held"
By K.M.M.

I Feel Good

Your words are a lullaby in harsh times,
To be held in your arms will be eternal to me.

I'm held in contempt to attempt wordless love,
If I had one wish it would be to fly the sky wander less with you.

For love there would be nothing more,
If you died and went to heaven.

I'd crawl through every puddle,
The only warmth I would need would be
    your name etched into my soul.

I'd always be by your side,
On the frontlines fighting for your memory.

Fighting for our love, our passion, our glory,
I would take the punishment of Limbo, to
    hold your hand one more time.

My Celestial Box

The years I spent loving you have been ground
    into a substance soft to the touch,
I spent those years crafting my celestial box.
The box in which I will leave my heart of warm love for you,
To feast upon with lavish squeals,
Of sentimental yells and pleas.
The almost rich entities that will help regain your sanity,
The astounding becomes old when you open my box.
The stars fall and countless wishes fly through me,
It's almost like it was not supposed to be.
Your smiling shatters the cold ice that's covering me,
Driving me upwards into the light.

"Box"
By K.M.M

Sand

Eyes locked,
With your arms around my neck,
I reach to kiss your light pink lips.
Your eyes cry for more, my eyes cry for love,
Your eyes go blank and you shatter in my arms.
Into a thousand little grains of sand lost in the sea,
I wish I could find you again.

But I know it's pointless to try,
I only wish I had worshipped every little thing we had;
I can't go on without you anymore.
Even with all the memories we shared,

I feel like it all means nothing without you.
You're the only girl who could tame my body,
And the only one who lies in my soul eternally.
Your voice compels me to stay,
And never leave our sanctuary of love.
I will never leave; I will wait for you, my love.

Fire

Dance within the fire,
But don't let it consume
The whisper of the trees.
So give up our differences and become mesmerized.
I don't know your fate but I know mine,
To escape the desire to steal her heart
And watch her ghost enter the smoke.
Fire consumes and ends all,
But starts new life at the end of the purge.
It screams with a crackle and pop to end all,
Is this divinity or just a fraud?
Wait till the organ of the church plays,
Then we shall see the end,
And the beginning.

"The Beginning of our New Life"
By K.M.M.

An Enormous Thanks to the Artists, Photographers and Editors who have donated their time and work in order to help visualize my words. Below you will find a list of each person who has helped me, each piece that is theirs and their contact information.

Name	Work	Contact Information
Alana Igbe	1) Front cover "The Red" 2) Back cover "Shadows"	alana_igbe@hotmail.com alanaigbe.wixcom/photography
Sean Henry	1) Chillin on the Cliff 2) Dark Angel 3) Devil on my Shoulder 4) Hand Writing 5) Spray Can	seanhenry1@mac.com
Tamara Lewis	1) I'm finally Free	
Tamarra Kirkpatrick	1) Razor Blade	tckirkpatrick92@gmail.com
Romario Dunn	1) Surrounded by Spirits	
Lahayma Robinson	1) A Couple Talking 2) A Note	
Karieta Robinson	1) Heartbroken 2) Reaching Out	
K.M.M.	1) Moon 2) A Sketch of Tammy 3) Hands Held 4) The Beginning of our New Life 5) Box 6) Dedication Photo	kandykittykat@yahoo.com

Cayce Mollycheck	Editor	case.cook@yahoo.com
Laurie E. Teleford Mahfood	Editor	
Jay Mahfood	Editor	jmahfood42@gmail.com

Printed in the United States
By Bookmasters